P9-BZW-528

A Patchwork of Programs 2
For Women's Ministries

A Patchwork of 2 PROGRAMS
For Women's Ministries

NORA BURDETT & KAREN KELLER

Beacon Hill Press of Kansas City
Kansas City, Missouri

ISBN 083-411-7746

Printed in the
United States of America

Cover Design: Marie Tabler
Inside Line Art: Karen Keller
            Karen Heidler

Library of Congress Cataloging-in-Publication Data

Burdett, Nora, 1947-
    A patchwork of programs 2 for women's ministries / Nora Burdett and Karen Keller.
        p. cm.
    ISBN 0-8341-1774-6 (pbk.)
    1. Church work with women.   2. Christian women—Religious life.   I. Keller, Karen.
    II. Title.   III. Title: Patchwork of programs two for women's ministries.
    BV4445.B87   1999
    259'.082—dc21   99-18664
                                                                          CIP

10   9   8   7   6   5   4   3   2   1

Dedication

We thank the Lord Jesus Christ for loving us, saving us, and giving us loving and supportive families who have enhanced every aspect of our lives.

We dedicate this book to
The Keller girls, Joahna and Nanette,
and their husbands, and to
The Burdett boys, Sean and Scott.

To **Joahna,** whose spiritual dedication is shown as she and her family serve the Lord in Japan as missionaries. She has blessed us with two grandsons here and little Meagan in heaven.

To **Nanette,** whose spiritual depth and enthusiasm for life is shown in the training of the four grandsons she has given us, and in the mentor she is to other women.

To **Scott,** who has always made sure that our sense of humor was in good working order. He is a survivor of some tough times and a wonderful man of God in the making.

To **Sean,** who is living proof that with God nothing is impossible, and that He can turn a disability into our greatest asset. He exemplifies the very love of God.

Contents

Acknowledgments

A great big bundle of thank-yous to those who encouraged us when we said "never again" and to those who nurtured and prayed for us when we were spent. A few of those vital links in our writing ministry chain are:

Ken and Sam—our ever-patient and helpful husbands of 30 and 41 years respectively.

Dell and Brendan—for the use of the seaside getaway at Zilzie.

Audrey, Christine, and Doreen—for hours of proofreading.

Karen and Sean—who lost and retrieved a vital part of our manuscript.

Dad, Ed May—for computer time and supplies.

Vicki Day—for use of her office.

Norma Gillming—mentor extraordinaire.

Introduction

"Anything worth doing is worth doing well." Purposeful planning is paramount to the success of any project. Here are a few things to consider when planning your function:

Purpose	Audience Needs
Place	Promotion
Time	Coordinators
Cost	Acknowledgments
Speaker	

Use these complete programs or take ideas to use as a springboard to enhance your own ideas.

Don't forget to "count the cost" (budget) and then see if you can sell any of your decorations to recover some of the expense for the next function.

Remember that all artwork in this book is made to be enlarged or copied and used, provided credit is given to the authors for its use.

These programs aren't restricted for use in church. Try using them for your school, office, or neighborhood party. Have fun!

BERRY SPECIAL FRIENDS

Keep alive the mentoring principles of Titus 2:3-5

OPTION

Women's Daytime Seminar

DECORATIONS

Tables

Navy and white check tablecloths with red napkins. At each place setting alternate red and navy cardboard folders that will hold seminar information for the day.

Centerpieces

Berry baskets (See Resources.)

Program Cover

Navy and red folders hold forms for Berries and Blossoms.

Name Tags

(See Appendix, Items 1-B and 1-C.)

SPECIAL FEATURES

Songs

"Make New Friends but Keep the Old" (See Resources.)
"What a Friend We Have in Jesus"

Testimonies

Voices from the Past—Bible women speak to women today with a few words of wisdom. (See Resources.)
From Past Participants in the Mentoring Program (See Resources.)

Some Bible Examples

(See Resources.)

Suggested Activities

(See Resources.)

Jam Sessions

Berries: How to Be a Mentor (See Resources.)
Blossoms: How to Be Mentored (See Resources.)

Forms

(See Resources.)

Skit

More than a Bucket of Berries (See Resources.)

Game

The Perfect Friend (See Resources.)

DEVOTION

(See Resources.)

FOOD

Brunch

Low-fat blueberry muffins, berry (herbal) teas, berry jam

Lunch

Polynesian chicken salad with raspberry dressing, assorted bread rolls, fresh berry tarts, berry punch (See Resources.)

RESOURCES

Centerpieces

On lightweight cardboard copy two basket patterns for each centerpiece. (See Appendix, Item 1-A.) Score across line at the bottom of baskets. Fold each base under, then overlap and secure with tape or glue. Staple or glue top of handles together and add a bow if you wish. You may want to color the berries.

Song

Make New Friends but Keep the Old

(old folk tune)

Make new friends,
But keep the old.
One is silver,
And the other gold.

Testimonies

Voices from the Past

(Prerecord ladies speaking the following parts.
Introduce the recordings as follows)

We have been able to secure on tape some of the most remarkable testimonies you have ever heard. We are actually going to take you back in time, and I mean right back, for a glimpse into the lives of some of the women we have known about for many years. Someone defined a mentor as "someone who has gone a little farther down the road than you." Well, these women are centuries down the road from us, but the lessons they want to share are just as important for us today as they were then. Listen to them and learn well.

SARAH (Genesis 16): I am Sarah, wife of Abraham, mother of Isaac. God said He would give us a son, but He had waited so long that it seemed humanly impossible for me to conceive. I took matters into my own hands and gave my handmaid, Hagar, to my husband to bear him a son. She did. His name was Ishmael, who became the father of the Arab nations. I would like to warn you of the consequences of being the ruling personality in your home. I was so impatient that I tried to take matters into my own hands. Our ways are never better than waiting on God and letting Him accomplish things in His own time. I had so much trouble waiting and believing God, and now the whole world suffers as a result of my mistake.

REBEKAH (Genesis 25:28—27:46): I am Rebekah, wife of Isaac. We had two boys, Jacob and Esau. Though they were twins, they were very different. Jacob was my favorite, while Isaac favored Esau. I encouraged my son Jacob to be dishonest, and he deceived his brother by stealing his birthright. The bitterness between them from that day caused Jacob to flee, and I never saw him again. I want to caution you about playing favorites with your children and teaching them to be deceptive even in little ways. It brought so much trouble into our family as a result of my doing these things.

LEAH (Genesis 29—30): I am Leah, first wife of Jacob. Seven days after our marriage, Jacob also took my sister, Rachel, as his wife. He always loved her more. Polygamy was a common practice in my day, so I had to share my husband with another wife. Even though that condition probably does not exist for you, your marriage may not have the love in it that you want. I know how that feels, but I am glad I stayed faithful and made the best of my marriage anyway.

RUTH (Ruth 1—4): My name is Ruth, daughter-in-law of Naomi. My husband died, leaving me as a young widow. I had heard my husband and his family speak of their God, and I knew my only hope was to follow my mother-in-law back to her country. How glad I am that God put this godly woman in my life and gave me the wisdom to follow her guidance. May you have the same success with your Berry Special Friend.

MARY (Luke 1—2): I am Mary, mother of the Lord Jesus Christ. I was what you would call an unwed mother. In my day I could have been stoned to death. Even my fiancé didn't understand. My cousin was a godly woman, and she took me in. She confirmed what I already knew—that God was doing a special work in my life. So when troubles seem too hard to bear, look for a godly woman who can encourage you to keep on keeping on.

SAPPHIRA (Acts 5:1, 8-10): My name is Sapphira, wife of Ananias. My husband and I were concerned about the poor, but we also realized there was a way we could gain great honor and admiration from our fellow Christians. We devised a plan to sell our property and give only part of the money to the Church while making it look like we had given it all. After all, we thought we needed to look out for ourselves too. I wish I had left a better example for you. I should have tried to persuade my husband to do what was right and to tell the truth rather than a lie. Instead I was selfish and agreed to the devious plan. As a result, we paid with our lives.

LOIS (2 Timothy 1:5): My name is Lois, and I am Timothy's grandmother. God was able to use my grandson in a great way partly because I shared my practical faith with his mother, Eunice, and then with him. Because of that training he was chosen to serve with the great apostle Paul and was said to be like-minded to him. Use the time with your grandchildren and other family members and friends to make a difference in their walk with the Lord. You are never too old to do this.

From Past Participants in the Mentoring Program

If you have done a mentoring program before or if someone in your group has been involved in one before, have her give a testimony as to the benefits and results of the program in her life. Use a mentor and someone who has been mentored if you can.

Devotion

Mentoring Program—"Berries and Blossoms"

Mentors are the "Berries"—mature, sweet, fruitful, and useful. Those to be mentored are the "Blossoms"—young, promising, developing fruit. Read Ps. 78 and Titus 2:3-5 together before starting.

Most everyone feels inadequate to be a mentor. Most people feel as though they need one. Remember, someone once said a mentor is "one who has gone down the road a little farther than you." This program is all about looking out for the needs of others and encouraging one another. An effective women's ministry is the mothering aspect in the Church. It is about growing together to become more Christlike. Christ is the real Teacher; we are all the pupils.

Older women teaching younger women is commanded in the Word of God. It is not an option. Titus 2:3-5. Develop your own adaptation of the following devotion.

1. Older women are to be holy, honest, sober teachers of good things.

2. Young women are to be taught to be sober, to love their husbands and children, to be self-controlled, pure, busy at home, kind and submissive to their own husbands.

3. The result is that "the Word of God be not blasphemed." More people would hold the Christian life as well as the Word of God in higher regard if Christians lived the way they should live.

In this program you will be matched with another woman for one year. You will need to meet together at least once a month and keep in touch at least once a week. **(A note for leaders: You should keep in touch with each of your mentors once a month and pray for them and their ministry.)**

Some Biblical Examples

Naomi and Ruth
Eunice and Lois
Elizabeth and Mary
David and Jonathan
Barnabas and Saul
Aquila/Priscilla and Apollos

Suggested Activities

Bible study, lunch, outings (museums, picnics, parks, craft shows, seminars, etc.), walking, shopping, tennis, golf, exhibitions, a cup of tea or coffee at home. **Share this list in each of the Jam Sessions.**

Jam Sessions

Berries: How to Be a Mentor

A. Mentoring demands a commitment to a person and a process. Be committed to meet regularly, share with each other, and pray for each other.

B. A mentor is a friend with practical experiences to share; one who stands on the authority of God's Word.

C. A mentor is usually the older of the two people in the arrangement—or certainly the more spiritually mature. Be prepared that the one you mentor may become greater than you (Barnabas and Saul).

D. Mentoring will demand of you godliness, wisdom, experience, and availability. It is a full-time, personal relationship, not a nine-to-five job.

E. Mentoring usually has a time limit—one year at a time is best. Usually it ends, but sometimes a friendship is formed for life.

F. Mentoring is fulfilling because it enables you to help others grow, succeed, and become confident while it assures that your life keeps on impacting others.

G. To be a great mentor, you don't have to be famous, just willing.

H. One weakness can be that we only affirm and never confront issues with those we mentor. Balance confrontation with kindness.

I. Be transparent.

J. Have reasonable expectations.

Blossoms: How to Be Mentored

A. Mentoring demands a commitment to a person and a process. Be committed to meet regularly, share with each other, and pray for each other.

B. Let your mentor know what you want to learn.

C. Be willing to change and to listen to constructive criticism.

D. Be prepared to set some life goals and to be held accountable for them.

E. Contact your mentor from time to time; don't make her do all the work. To have a friend, be a friend.

F. Be transparent.

G. Be prepared to be affirmed and confronted with things that need to be developed and changed.

H. You will be stretched through mentoring.

I. You need to be honest, open, teachable, and appreciative.

J. Have reasonable expectations.

Forms
(See Appendix, Items 1-D, 1-E, 1-F.)

These forms should be in the folder on the table when the ladies arrive. Make copies of the "Berry Special Friends" questionnaire in both blue and pink. Copy "For Berries" sheets in blue and "For Blossoms" sheets in pink. Place the blue forms for Berries in the navy folders and pink forms for Blossoms in the red folders. Add a couple of blank sheets in each folder for taking notes. Folders can be decorated with berry stickers.

Skit

More than a Bucket of Berries
by Nora Burdett and Karen Keller

Characters:
    MABEL: *older friend*
    AUDREY: *younger friend*

Props:
    Infant car seat/carrier
    2 small plastic or metal buckets

Setting:

(Read by Narrator) Mabel, who is in her late 50s, gave out the word at church that she had a very large blackberry bush heavily laden with fruit to be given away for those willing to pick it themselves. Audrey is a young woman, new in the church, who has come to pick fruit.

AUDREY *(carrying doll in car seat, she calls out as she knocks on the screen door)*: Anybody home?

MABEL: I'm coming. Hi, come on in. I am so glad that you have come to get some of these blackberries. Aside from them making such a mess, I really hate to see them going to waste. *(Peeks into infant carrier at baby)* Look at this baby. He is so cute. Boys always look like angels when they are asleep. What is his name?

AUDREY: Jonathan. I was so glad that he fell asleep in the car coming over. He has been fussy all day.

MABEL: Well, let's set him over here so we can hear him if he cries. I'll get some buckets, and we'll get those berries picked before he wakes up.

(They pretend to walk outside and start picking berries and putting them in the bucket.)

AUDREY: I want to bake a pie with some of the blackberries. Bill says his mother made such good ones, and he is hungry for one. Yesterday in church, when we heard that you had some berries, he looked at me and smiled. I knew what he was thinking. He wanted a pie, but he wouldn't ask me to make one because he knows I nearly have nightmares when it comes to making pie crusts. But I'll give it a try.

MABEL: Well if you need one, I have a "never fail" pie crust recipe I can give you. But why don't you make it easy on yourself and go get one of those frozen ones at the supermarket. They're really good. Bill will never know the difference.

AUDREY: I think I might just do that. I do want him to enjoy it. *(Reflective pause)* You know, things are different than I thought they would be before I got married.

MABEL: I remember feeling that way myself, and that was 35 years ago.

AUDREY *(yawns)*: Since Jonathan has come into our lives, I can never seem to get enough sleep.

MABEL: Do you ever try to sleep while the baby is napping?

AUDREY: I often feel like it, but I try to use that time to clean. Bill is pickier about the house than I thought he would be.

MABEL: You know what I realized early in my marriage? *(Gives a little chuckle)* If you find out what is really important to your man and keep those things done, you can let a lot of the other things slip on really busy days. That way you can even fit in a nap when you are dragging. Then you will be in better spirits to give him some attention when he comes home.

AUDREY: That's a really good idea. *(The two quietly pick fruit for a little while.)* Bill will be so proud of me for saving money by picking this fruit today. We have been married two years now, and I sometimes feel he still doesn't really trust me in money matters. But I really do try to stay within the budget.

MABEL: Building trust, especially about money, takes time. I am sure in his line of work that Bill has seen plenty of women who can throw money out the back door with a teaspoon faster than their husbands can bring it home with a shovel. *(Both laugh.)* It takes time for a couple to completely trust each other.

AUDREY: We were married six months before he even gave me my own set of keys to his truck. Even then I was only allowed to drive it on very special occasions.

MABEL: A man's car—or truck—is a precious possession to him. I think of them as toys for big boys.

AUDREY: Someone ran into the back of the precious pickup and scratched it the other day. I was so glad he was driving and not me.

MABEL: After the first scratch, the second is not so serious. You're home free now.

AUDREY *(looks at her watch):* Oh, my goodness, it's getting late and Bill is coming home early and I forgot to lay out anything to defrost. He is always hungry when he gets home.

MABEL: My experience has been that men are always hungry, period. What is the fastest thing that you could cook that he really likes?

AUDREY: Well, he brags on my pancakes. But for dinner?

MABEL: Why not? Cook up some bacon and eggs and make lots of pancakes and warm the maple syrup. Tell him that you thought it would be a nice change.

AUDREY: Well, I hardly ever fix them for breakfast because he is always rushing off to early meetings. He might just really enjoy it. Thanks so much for the blackberries—and all the good advice. How did you get to be so wise?

MABEL: I'm not really so wise. I have just walked down life's road a little longer than you have.

AUDREY: Well, it has been a real treat meeting you. I'm sorry I have to run.

MABEL: I'll carry the berries out while you get the baby. Let me just wash my hands first. *(Moves away to the imaginary sink to wash her hands and thinks out loud)* I think maybe I was of some help to that girl today. Maybe I'm not all used up as I was beginning to feel. *(Dries her hands and returns to Audrey)*

MABEL *(hesitantly):* Audrey, would you like to come over sometime for a cup of tea and a chat?

AUDREY: Oh, Mabel, I was hoping you would ask. I would really love to. Thank you.

(Both freeze, then lights dim as they exit.)

Game

The Perfect Friend

This game is for four people, so divide into groups of four. Take a sheet of white paper for each group and fold it the same direction into four equal parts. The first person should draw the head and neck of a lady, then fold that part of the paper back over so the next person cannot see what is drawn, leaving only a small bit of the neck for the next person to connect to. The second person draws from the neck to the waist, folds back her paper leaving only a bit of the waistline showing for the third person. The third person draws from the waist to the knees and the fourth person from the knees to the feet in the same manner as above.

When everyone is finished, they should unfold their paper for all to see just what the Perfect Friend looks like. Emphasize that good friends come in all shapes and sizes, just like these.

Food

Polynesian Chicken Salad with Raspberry Dressing

2 heads of lettuce (use special varieties like butter, mignonette, etc.)
1 small Spanish onion
2 lbs. cooked, skinless, boneless chicken breasts, cut into bite-sized
    pieces
2 mangoes, peeled and sliced (canned mangoes or peaches can be used)
⅔ c. toasted pecan halves
Dressing:
½ c. cold pressed, extra-virgin olive oil
½ c. frozen or canned raspberries with juice
2 tbsp. white vinegar
2 tsp. sesame oil
4 tsp. honey
½ tsp. Tabasco sauce
salt and pepper

Wash, dry, and tear lettuce and place in mixing bowl along with onion, mango, and pecans. Refrigerate until ready for dressing. Toss with salad dressing just before serving. Place chicken pieces on top of salad and serve.

Prepare dressing by placing all ingredients in screw-top jar and shake well. Toss with salad just prior to serving. If dressing is too lumpy, you might prefer to process it in the blender until smooth. Serves 6 to 8.

CREATIVE ENCOUNTER
Learn how to use what you don't know you have

OPTIONS

Ladies

Couples' Night

Teacher Training

All-Day Seminar

DECORATIONS

Tables

(See Resources.)

Name Tags

(See Resources.)

SPECIAL FEATURES

Game

Proverbs Quiz (See Appendix, Item 2-A.)

The "Great Idea" Hat

(See Resources.)

Skit

The Diagnosis (See Resources.)

FOOD

Whole wheat pita chips and salsa or hummus (healthy, low-fat)
(See Resources.)
Create an original snack to bring (along with recipe, of course)
Create-your-own: ice cream sundae, pizza, sandwich, or snack.
(Be sure to allow for those on low-calorie or sugar-free diets.)

INSTRUCTIONS FOR THE PROGRAM

The purpose of this program is to help people see, in a fun way, just how creative they can be. There are a number of exercises given to do as a group that will illustrate each point. Pick and choose which ones you want to do according to your time frame. Be sure to pick at least one to go along with each of the "creativity booster" pills. Start with the name tags and pass the "Great Idea" hat around each time someone comes up with a good idea. Here is a suggested schedule:

Introduction

The "Great Idea" Hat

Name Tags

Table Decorations

Skit

Creative Encounter "Support Group"

Conclusion

Food

INTRODUCTION FOR THE PROGRAM (Leader)

I. God is the only true Creator. He made everything out of nothing. Eccles. 1:9-10 tells us there is nothing new under the sun, but there are endless ways to create new ideas and things out of combinations of what has been created. The old adage "necessity is the mother of invention" is proven when we come up with an answer to a particular problem or need.

II. Christ is the same yesterday, today, and forever, but our world and people keep changing. There is always a need for fresh, new ideas. When you get an idea, do something with it as soon as you can. Every idea has a "use by" date. Very few, if any, have a long shelf life. Those you don't develop will become obsolete.

Exercise: Have the group come up with several "inventions" that are no longer used. (Examples: button hooks, telegrams, mimeograph machines) Then have them think of some newer inventions. (Examples: microwaves, computers, answering machines) Creative thinking means seeing and thinking differently.

Exercise: Show this picture and ask what the group sees. They should be able to see a duck, a rabbit, and a man, and maybe more.

III. Do you think you are creative? How many said "NO! I am not creative." You are conditioning yourself to not be creative. You are more creative than you think.

Exercise: Remember back to the last time you created something of any kind. What was it, and what caused you to come up with it?

We need to understand how our brain works—it has two sides. The left side is logical and rational, while the right side is creative. It is important to learn to let the right side have freedom to create and use its capabilities before the left side gets involved and judges with its logic. Creative ideas need to be workable but may never be thought of if we let the rational left side control all our thinking. After an idea is born it can be directed, adapted, and made workable by the left side of the brain. We need both sides working together. Our mind is a storehouse of resources to use creatively.

RESOURCES

The "Great Idea" Hat

Make the hat according to directions. *Every time you do an "exercise," give the hat to the person with the best idea.* If a whole table had the idea, let them choose who should wear the hat. Be sure the hat passes around all evening, as an award for the best ideas in each exercise.

Instructions for Making "Great Idea" Hat—Glue creative motif (see Appendix, Item 2-B) onto a 2" wide band that is long enough to adjust to any size head. Highlight stars with gold glitter paint and highlight the lightning with silver glitter paint. Attach 2" Velcro strips on ends of the band.

Name Tags

Exercise: Everyone is given a name tag. (See Appendix, Item 2-C.) On the top line they should write their name, and underneath is the phrase "I WISH _____." Each person is to fill in the blank on his or her own name tag. Be creative and think of something "way out" or "fun"—maybe something that has always been a secret desire. This is *not* to be something spiritual but something from our inner self that would make us very excited.

Table Decorations

Exercise: Give each table a box of unusual things to create their own table decoration. Ideas for contents of box: paper roll, yarn, old toothbrush, paper plate, paper cup, jar lid, colored paper, toothpicks, and so on. Tools for each table: glue stick, scissors, and colored pages. (This will get their creative juices going.)

LEADER: Now let's look in on someone who is having more than a little trouble with creativity.

Skit

The Diagnosis
by Nora Burdett and Karen Keller

Characters:
> DR. I. DEA: *dressed in white lab coat, wearing dark-rimmed glasses, speaking in a European accent; a pad, pen, telephone, and kaleidoscope on his desk*
> MRS. I. M. DRAINED: *patient*

Props: Brain X ray (made from instructions), pill bottle

Setting: Inside the doctor's office. The doctor is sitting in his chair, looking out his window, through his kaleidoscope. A voice announces his next patient.

VOICE: Dr. I. Dea, your 4:00 patient, Mrs. I. M. Drained, is here to see you.

DOCTOR: Okeydokey. Beam her on up, Sandy.

PATIENT *(enters, adjusting her clothes and looking somewhat startled—as though she has been beamed up):* That was interesting!

DOCTOR *(turning around from window and laying kaleidoscope down):* Now, what can I do for you today?

PATIENT: Well, Doc, it's like this. I am afraid that there might be something wrong with my brain. I haven't had a creative thought for a long, long time. Do you think you can help me?

DOCTOR: What are the symptoms you've been experiencing?

PATIENT: I feel dried up, empty, drained. It's as though something has just sucked all the color right out of my world.

DOCTOR: Oh, dear. It sounds serious.

PATIENT: What do you mean, serious? How serious? *(Leans toward the DOCTOR's desk)* How long do I have, Doc?

DOCTOR: I won't be able to tell until I get the results from your multidimensional cranialgram.

PATIENT: Oh, that sounds painful!

DOCTOR: Nonsense. *(Looking over the top of his glasses)* It's an X ray.

PATIENT: Why didn't you say so?

DOCTOR: Just slip around the corner to the "Quick as a Flash" Radiology Unit, and bring me back the big picture, and then we'll see what's happening up there in that mysterious brain of yours.

PATIENT *(leaves and returns immediately with large poster board with cranialgram on it):* Well, that was painless enough, and I am at least relieved to see that I still have a brain.

(Instructions for making cranialgram: Enlarge outline of head with brain on poster board [see Appendix, Item 2-Ca]. Color left side blue, right side red.)

DOCTOR *(sets "X ray" up where it can be seen by all; studies it for a moment):* Ah, yes . . . but . . . oh me . . . Uh huh!

PATIENT: Doctor, please tell me. I can take it. I want the truth, even if it's bad.

DOCTOR: Well, it is bad. But it is also fixable. Let me show you some things on this X ray. *(Walk over together to the brain X ray.* DOCTOR *begins pointing to different areas.)* Now here we have your brain, which is made up of two identical parts. One side is blue, and it is called the left side of the brain. This side looks perfectly fine. It is your rational, judgmental, logical side. It even seems to be a bit larger than normal. It must be working overtime.

Now the red side, on the other hand, is the creative part of your brain. This is the imaginative, inspirational, warm, excitable, *(speaks louder and faster)* wild, bold, daring, playful, lively, fertile . . . Oh, you get the idea *(pause),* don't you? This whole side is a little smaller than normal. And look at that spot there, it is starting to dry up. And look what else. Oh my, right here is the biggest problem. It's locked up!

PATIENT: Is there anything you can do for me, Doc?

DOCTOR: Oh yes, yes, yes! Oh yes, oh yes! Come here while I explain. *(Both return to their seats.)* First of all, let me ask you a question. Do you think that you are a creative person?

PATIENT: That's why I'm here. I already told you, I'm not.

DOCTOR: That is what has caused the big lockup. Why, even the Bible says in Prov. 23:7 that "as he thinketh in his heart, so is he" (KJV). You have put that lock on yourself by wrong thinking. The first thing you must do is realize that anyone can unlock his or her creativity. The brain is a storehouse of resources to be used creatively. Scientists tell us that at best we only use 10 percent of the old gray matter in a lifetime. If you believe you can be creative, it will be like loosening that lock with a crowbar. Free it. Let it loose to percolate some imaginative ideas.

PATIENT *(slowly):* I think I can. *(With more thought)* I think I can. *(As though a bright light has gone off in her head)* I think I can . . . think . . . creatively.

DOCTOR: I believe you have loosened the lock already. Now you must nourish that right side of your brain so that it can function properly with the left side. Creative ideas need to be workable but must first be thought of, so we can't let the rational left side control *all* our thinking. After an idea is born in the right side it can be directed, adopted, and made workable by the left side of the brain. You see, *(sings this)* "You can't have one without the other . . ." and be relatively normal, that is. Our mind is a storehouse of resources to use creatively. So, I am going to give you this little bottle of pills called Time-Release Creativity Boosters. I also want you to go to a special Creative Encounter Support Group, which is ready to meet right now. They will be explaining just how to use these four tablets tonight. I believe you are well on your way to a cure.

PATIENT: Oh, Doctor, I just don't know how to thank you.

DOCTOR: Hurry on now. I must get back to my kaleidoscope. I think I might just be close to discovering the genetic makeup of the worry virus.

LEADER: Dr I. Dea has given us a lot to think about on the subject of being creative. It is so true that we need to allow both sides of the brain to function as they were designed to do. Let's go to the Creative Encounter Support Group where we will take Dr I. Dea's prescription to help us continue to think creatively.

INSTRUCTIONS FOR TIME-RELEASE CREATIVITY BOOSTERS

On a sheet of poster board, enlarge bottle design. (See Appendix, Item 2-D.) Using four balloons as giant "pills," write on a small piece of paper one of the four messages given below and slip one inside each balloon. Blow up the balloons to the size that looks best on your bottle, then cut small slits in the poster board at each spot where you will place a balloon. Slip the tied mouth of each balloon into the indicated places inside the bottle design on the poster board. Label the bottle Time-Release Creativity Boosters.

I. Break the first balloon "tablet" and read the message on the paper inside: **Metaphors—they link old knowledge with new. They break the rules of logic and carry new concepts through normal thinking barriers to stimulate the mind. God used metaphors to give understanding.**

Exercise 1: Hand out Proverbs quiz (see Appendix, Item 2-A) for people to do, using their Bibles if necessary. Draw a line from the metaphor to its meaning. Here are the correct answers: **1-G, 2-H, 3-I, 4-J, 5-B, 6-C, 7-D, 8-A, 9-E, 10-F.**

Exercise 2: Break up the group into pairs or small groups, and have each group write or draw a metaphor of one of the following:
Life is like _____.
Church is like _____.
Example: Life is like a bowl of cherries—pits and all.

II. Break second balloon "tablet" and read the message on paper inside: Looking at things from a "foolish" point of view can trigger creativity. (Read 1 Cor. 3:18-19.) **The foolish (or simple) point of view helps us see things from a different vantage point. Looking at a problem in an obscure, irrelevant, or irrational way can help us see solutions otherwise overlooked. Reversing your point of view or taking a contrary position in a common proverb can help gain insight otherwise missed.**

Illustration: "A chain is no stronger than its weakest link." Now reverse that view: A weak link can be a good thing. Many times people design a weakness into a system just as a safety precaution. The most familiar one is the circuit breaker. It is designed to save the entire system when there is an overload, the premise being that you just flip a switch rather than replace the whole system.

Exercise: Take one or all three of these common sayings and by reversing the meaning see what new insights you can get.

A. **"To err is human, to forgive divine."**
(For Leader: Easily forgiving over and over again when the person has no desire to change isn't helping them. To err can be an excuse for not disciplining yourself to try harder.)

B. **"Cleanliness is next to godliness."**
(For Leader: Getting dirty from hard work is good and scriptural.)

C. **"Why worry when you can pray."**
(For Leader: Worry can be concern to make us search for an answer. Expecting God to do it all can be an excuse if we are not willing to do our part.)

III. Break third balloon "tablet" and read the message on paper inside: Learning from nature can help us be more creative.

- **Velcro was developed by examining how burrs cling to material.**
- **The squid and how it propels itself through the waters triggered the invention of the jet plane.**
- **Snake fangs gave birth to the idea of the hypodermic needle.**

Exercise 1: Have the group brainstorm and write down how plants spread their seeds and propagate themselves. The leader can give one or two illustrations from the following list:

- Seeds are carried in bird droppings
- Wind carries some like parachutes, others like propellers, others sail
- Falling to the ground
- Water
- Fire
- Pods
- Nuts
- Insects
- From original plants
- Fruit—rolls away or is carried away and eaten later

Exercise 2: Now take list from brainstorming session and apply to ways the gospel could be spread. Most ways are applicable in some form.

IV. Break fourth balloon "tablet" and read the message on paper inside: Imagination—**It is "intelligence having fun." We did this best as children, then someone said, "Grow up," and "Get Real." Imagination was curbed.**

A. Ways to use imagination

1. Become the idea; what if you wanted to improve a soft drink and its packaging? Become the soft drink. How do I taste? How could I be more attractive to others? How can I get people to notice me?

   Example: To develop his early concepts of relativity, Einstein imagined he was an elevator falling through space at the speed of light. Imagination can transport you by using one idea to trigger a better one and so on until you get a really good, workable idea.

2. Use "What if?" imagination.

   Example: What if chairs were made out of mushrooms? How could a chair be improved by thinking like this?

3. How would someone else from another area of expertise do it?

   Example: How would General Patton run a girls' deportment class?

Exercise 1: Brainstorm: If Walt Disney or Steven Spielberg were the Sunday School superintendent of your church, what would Sunday School be like? (For the leader only: Sunday School would be well-organized, friendly, fun, full of choices, imaginative in teaching facts, first class, well-staffed, with good food.)

Exercise 2: Let's wonder about one of the following. Brainstorm one of these two thoughts and share ideas at the end.

A. **"Hope is a little feathered thing, that perches in the soul and sings a tune with no words and never stops at all."**

   1. I wonder if the tune had words, what would they be? Why do you think some people feel hopeless when hope's tune is always playing?

   2. 1 Cor. 13:13 lists hope as one of the big three, along with faith and love. Why is it so important? Why is love greater than hope?

   3. 1 Pet. 3:15 tells us to be ready to give an account of the hope that we have. How can we do this?

B. **"If in your heart there is a green bough, a singing bird will come."**

   1. I wonder what the green bough would be?

   2. What would the singing bird be?

Exercise 3: Give each table a familiar Bible character and a well-known modern-day person, and have them imagine what a conversation between the two would be like.

1. I wonder what they would talk about.

2. I wonder what they have in common with each other.

3. I wonder what insight could be gained from this conversation.

Examples: Adam and Eve with the president and his wife; Moses with your pastor; Paul with a missionary your church supports; Esther with a woman in politics locally or nationally.

Exercise 4: Look at a boomerang and its purpose. What can we learn about life from boomerangs? What things does the Scripture say will return to us? How do these things in the Scripture affect us in our lives?

OPTIONAL EXERCISES FOR THIS PROGRAM OR AN ALL-DAY SEMINAR

1. Have groups write a song about being creative, set to a simple, familiar tune.

2. Get groups to draw or write on a large piece of butcher paper what they have learned about being creative. They can show their mural to the other groups.

LEADER: As a result of this evening I hope you will become more aware of your own creativity, and I encourage you to nourish it. We have only scratched the surface of the subject. Use the creative treasure the Lord has given each of you.

Food

Whole Wheat Pita Chips and Hummus or Salsa
(healthy, low-fat)

For whole wheat pita chips, buy whole wheat pita or pocket bread. Open it up completely, and cut into bite-size pieces. Place in a single layer on an ungreased cookie sheet and bake in a 250-degree oven for 15 minutes. Turn off oven at end of baking time and leave chips in oven to finish drying and crisping. You don't want them brown, just crisp.

When cool, store in airtight containers. Serve with salsa or hummus for a healthy, low-fat, low-sodium treat. They make great dippers for any dip and are wonderful broken a little smaller and sprinkled over salads—with fewer calories than normal croutons.

Hummus (Chickpea Dip)

8 oz. chickpeas (add 1 teaspoon soda and water to cover; soak overnight)
4-5 tbsp. tahini (buy at health food or specialty shops)
juice of 1½ lemons
2 tbsp. olive oil
2-3 cloves garlic, crushed
¼ tsp. paprika
½ tsp. salt
black pepper

Method:

1. Drain and rinse chickpeas. Put in large pan with plenty of fresh water. Bring to a boil and cook fiercely for 10 minutes. Reduce heat, remove scum, and simmer covered until soft, about 60 to 90 minutes, depending upon the age of the peas.

2. Drain thoroughly, reserving liquid, and grind to a fine powder using the grinding blade of food processor, mincer, or blender.

3. Add ¼ pint of reserved stock and blend to a stiff paste. You may need to add more stock. Add all other ingredients; mix thoroughly and leave to stand for at least 2 hours for the flavors to develop. Taste and season. Add more lemon juice if necessary.

4. Turn hummus into shallow dish. Just before serving, garnish with a trickle of olive oil (optional), lemon slices, and parsley. Serve with pita bread or whole wheat toast. Makes 1¼ pints.

DINOMANIA

The party even an ol' fossil will love

OPTIONS

Once-a-year birthday or anniversary party for all the church, office, school, neighborhood, senior citizens' group, club, etc.

DECORATIONS

Tables

Cover with tablecloths in bright green, pink, purple, and/or yellow. Cut different shapes of dino-footprints (see Appendix, Item 3-A) from black paper, place on each table, and sprinkle with confetti.

Centerpieces

Dinosaur sandwich boards. Use one or both pictures given to make sandwich boards for tables. (See Resources.)

Room Decorations

Clusters of bright balloons and streamers all over the room. Using a dinosaur coloring book, make a scrapbook by coloring in selected pages and putting your own captions on them. Keep in mind the person or persons you are honoring.

Program Cover

(See Appendix, Items 3-B—3-C.)

Name Tags

Using pattern (see Appendix, Item 3-D), write first name above the line, then age after "Dino-mite at _____." If guests have a problem with telling their age, let them fill in the blank with a hobby, talent, or such.

SPECIAL FEATURES

Songs

"Joy for Life" (See Resources.)
"Happy Birthday Song" (See Resources.)

Games

Roving Dinosaurs (See Resources.)
Dinosaur Spelling Bee (See Resources.)
Matching Dinos (See Resources.)
Junk-o-Saurus (See Resources.)
What's in a Name? (See Resources.)

Take-Home Favors

Every birthday party has presents. Have everyone bring something, preferably along the dinosaur theme, and exchange gifts.

DEVOTION

(See Resources.)

FOOD

Prehistoric Strata Sandwich (See Resources.)

RESOURCES

Centerpieces

Sandwich boards are double-sided with a 2½" base. Use lightweight cardboard in a bright color to go with your scheme. They should be approximately 6" to 8" high. Copy a different picture on each side. (See Appendix, Item 3-B or 3-C.)

Songs

Joy for Life

(This little song is sung to the tune of "Row, Row, Row Your Boat." Sing it in a round, going from one table to another, or dividing the group in half.)

Unlike the dinosaurs of old,
We are still around
Our feet are planted on the Rock
And joy for life resounds.

Happy Birthday Song

(Sing to the tune of "Happy Birthday to You.")

Happy birthday to you,
Happy birthday to me too,
Tonight all the dinosaurs,
Will celebrate with us too.

Games

Roving Dinosaurs
by Nora Burdett and Karen Keller

This game will require 14 people to play, 1 to tell the story, and 1 scorekeeper. Have two rows of seven chairs, facing each other. Seven people sit in each row, again facing each other. Starting from opposite ends, give one person on each side the same dinosaur name from the story. The story will need seven characters.

As the story below is told, whenever a player hears his or her dinosaur name mentioned (there will be one on each side), she must get up and run around his or her entire row of chairs and be reseated before the player on the other side. A scorekeeper is in charge of giving a point to each side who reaches the seat first. Any time the word "dinosaur" is mentioned, the entire team must run around their row of chairs and be reseated. The first team to be reseated receives 10 points. The winning team at the end is the one with the highest score.

The Players: Ken Kristosaurus (a boy) and Nancy Nychosaurus (a girl), Sara Sauropod (their neighbor), Isaac Iguanodon (the grocer), Bill Brachiosaurus (the baker), Arthur Ankylosaurus (an old fossil who's their friend), and the awful Tyrone Tyrannosaurus Rex.

The Story: <u>Ken Kristosaurus</u> and his friend <u>Nancy Nychosaurus</u> lived on the valley floor of Fantastic Park. They shared their valley home with many friends, like their neighbor, Sara Sauropod; Isaac Iguanodon, the grocer; Bill Brachiosaurus, the baker; and their very old friend, Arthur Ankylosaurus. Arthur Ankylosaurus was so old they sometimes called him a fossil. In their lush, green valley, everything was just perfect—well, almost everything. There was one creature they all feared, and his name was Tyrone Tyrannosaurus Rex.

Well, Arthur Ankylosaurus was about to celebrate a birthday, and it was a really big one. Ken Kristosaurus and Nancy Nychosaurus wanted to do something very special for him, so they decided to plan a surprise birthday party. They reminded all their friends to keep it a secret.

Ken Kristosaurus and Nancy Nychosaurus asked Sara Sauropod to help by writing out the invitations. She did just that and then gave them back to Nancy and Ken to mail to their friends. Isaac Iguanodon, the grocer, was given a list of supplies they needed, like candles, napkins, paper plates, and special junkasaurus food that all dinosaurs love. He ordered the supplies right away.

Next Ken Kristosaurus and Nancy Nychosaurus went to see the baker, Bill Brachiosaurus, and asked him to make a huge cake. "Remember to keep it a secret from Arthur Ankylosaurus," they said, "but more importantly, don't let Tyrone Tyrannosaurus Rex get wind of it. He would just love to find a bunch of dinosaurs having a celebration. He would have a party too, but he wouldn't be eating the birthday cake."

As the day of the party drew near, all the dinosaurs worked hard making the valley floor a festive place. They even hung a big banner that read, "Happy Birthday, Arthur Ankylosaurus, You Old Fossil."

On the day of the party Isaac Iguanodon came with all the things they had ordered. Bill Brachiosaurus brought the most beautiful birthday cake any of them had ever seen. Ken Kristosaurus, Nancy Nychosaurus, and Sara Sauropod put the finishing touches on the tables and wrapped the gift for Arthur Ankylosaurus. Then they heard some rumbling in the distance, and they knew that it was either thunder or Tyrone Tyrannosaurus Rex. Remembering how well they had kept their secret, they knew it must be thunder.

When everything was ready, the little group of dinosaurs decided to sit down and wait quietly for the rest of their friends to arrive. It got later and later and darker and darker, and no one came. Not even one dinosaur came. They were really getting worried. Sara Sauropod finally asked her friends when they mailed the invitations. Nancy Nychosaurus at once realized that neither of them had sent out the invitations. They had kept such a good secret that not even the guest of honor, Arthur Ankylosaurus, was there. Isaac Iguanodon and Bill Brachiosaurus suggested that all the dinosaurs enjoy the junkosaurus food anyway. Just as they were filling their plates, the rumbling they had heard earlier became really loud, and as a large shadow passed over them in the moonlight, they realized that they did indeed have an uninvited guest, Tyrone Tyrannosaurus Rex.

"How did you know about our party when we forgot to send out invitations?" the little group asked. "I can always smell a dinosaur party," said Tyrone Tyrannosaurus Rex. At that point all the dinosaurs ran for cover. When they were all safely away, they agreed that they were glad that their old friend Arthur Ankylosaurus hadn't come, because he couldn't move as fast as the rest of them anymore. In the distance they could hear Tyrone Tyrannosaurus Rex say in a defeated tone, "I came for a feast, then hoped for a snack. Now it looks like I'll just have to fast. This really was a surprise party after all."

Dinosaur Spelling Bee

Someone should read aloud these 20 dinosaur names while everyone else tries to spell them. This is a challenge even to the best spellers in the crowd. Pronunciation guide included to help you get your tongue around each beast.

Ankylosaurus (ang-kih-luh-SAWR-us)
Brachiosaurus (BREAK-ee-uh-SAWR-us)
Compsognathus (komp-so-NAY-thus)
Diplodocus (die-PLOD-uh-cus)
Hypsilophodon (hip-sih-LOF-uh-don)
Iguanodon (ig-GWAHN-uh-don)
Maiasaura (mah-ee-ah-SAWR-uh)
Supersaurus (su-per-SAWR-us)
Sauropod (SAWR-uh-pod)
Coelophysis (see-luh-FYE-sis)
Lystrosaurus (lie-struh-SAWR-us)
Plateosaurus (PLAY-tee-uh-SAWR-us)
Dimetrodon (die-MET-ruh-don)
Hypselosaurus (HIP-sih-luh-SAWR-us)
Kritosaurus (KRIT-uh-SAWR-us)
Anatasaurus (uh-NAT-uh-SAWR-us)
Hypacrosaurus (hie-PACK-ruh-SAWR-us)
Stenonychosaurus (stuh-NON-ick-uh-SAWR-us)
Micropachycephalosaurus (my-kro-PACK-ee-SEF-uh-luh-SAWR-us)
Parasaurolophus (PAR-uh-sawr-AHL-uh-fus)

Matching Dinos

Take pictures of 10 of the most common dinosaurs from a coloring book, encyclopedia, or off your computer, and place in a line on the wall. Number each picture. Give a scrambled list of dinosaur names covering the 10 on the wall. Have guests put the correct number by the name.

Junk-o-Saurus

Choose several "scientific teams" to reassemble the remains of some extinct creatures recently discovered in your area. Provide large cereal boxes, empty cardboard rolls from paper products, string, paper, cardboard, plastic, colored markers, scissors, glue, tape, and so forth. In 10 minutes see what kind of extinct creatures the teams can reassemble. Upon completion one member has to give the critter's name and a creative description to the audience. The winning team will not necessarily have the cutest dino, but the name and description will probably take the prize. (Prizes can be anything from dinosaur cookies and candy to dinosaur Band-Aids.)

What's in a Name?

Did you ever wonder how the dinosaurs got their names? Every name has a special meaning. Names were originally devised to describe people by their various characteristics. Let's start by having some fun with the dinosaur names listed below.

(Print out these words on sheets and pass out to guests. Invite people to see if they can describe themselves, someone at their table, or even their best friend using these Greek and Latin root words and their meanings. Keep it funny and light-hearted, not cruel. Examples: pachycephalo-plateopodosaurus—a thick-headed, flat-footed lizard; or compso-op-sosaurus—pretty-face lizard).

Word	Meaning	Word	Meaning
dino	terrible	saur	lizard
anato	duck	cephalo	head
ankylo	crooked	cerat, ceros	horn
anuro	tail	chasmo	opening
coeli	hollow	avi, avis	bird
bary	heavy	compso	pretty
brachio	arm	di, diplo	two
caudia	tail	segno	slow
centro	midway	docus	beam
don, dont	tooth	dryo	oak
gnathus	jaw	hadro	large
hypacro	below the top	hypselo, hypsi	high
ichthyo	fish	iguano	iguana
krito	chosen	lopho	crest, ridge
lystro	shovel	maia	good mother
masso	bulk, body	mega	large
metro	measure	micro	small
nycho	claw	opistho	backward
ops	face	pachy	thick
pacro	ridged	para	beside
physis	form	plateo	flat
plesio	ribbon	pod, ped	foot
proto	first	rex	king
spino	spine	stego	roof
steno	slender	super	superior
thero	summer	tri	three
troo	wound	tyranno	tyrant
ultra	extreme	urus	tail
veloci	speedy	vulcano	volcano

Devotion

Message from the Dinosaurs

Well, we learned that there certainly is a lot in a name, especially if you are a dinosaur. But what does the Bible have to say to us about our names. The names of people in the Bible often described their character. This was so important to God that He often changed a name as the person changed. Examples: Abram to Abraham, Sarai to Sarah, Jacob to Israel, Saul to Paul. Often converts on the mission field will change their name to that of a Bible character or someone they admire to show their acceptance of Christ. (See Prov. 22:1; Eccles. 7:1.)

We know that dinosaurs existed because their footprints and skeletons have been found in rock formations. If our feet are firmly planted on the Rock of Ages, our footprints will be there for others to follow one day as well. (See Ps. 27:5; 40:2.)

We can leave our footprints in this world by making a difference in the lives of others. "Touch the life of a child and you could change generations to come." (See Titus 2:7-8; James 5:10; 2 Cor. 9:2; 2 Thess. 3:9; 2 Tim. 1:5.)

Food

Prehistoric Strata Sandwich

Choose to make either individual sandwiches or one (or more, depending on size of your group) very large French bread stick, or something specially created by the baker, to create a dinosaur-sized sandwich, big enough to feed a crowd.

Simply take a wide variety of sandwich meats and cheese slices, and using dinosaur cookie cutters, cut shapes out of each. Cut the bread open and put your favorite spread on both halves. Lay ample crisp lettuce leaves on the bottom half, as well as fresh tomato slices, Spanish onion rings, and so forth. Lay the scraps left from the cutouts of meat and cheese down the center of the loaf, and lay the cut shapes along the edges. Make sure the shapes hang over the edge a little so they can be seen. Slice in individual serving sizes when you are ready to serve them.

Other Ideas

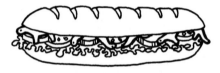

Brontosaurus Bake (any casserole), Spag-a-saurus (spaghetti, what else?), Baby Pterodactyl Wings (chicken wings), Mammoth Marbles (small baked potatoes drenched in melted butter and parsley flakes), Volcanic Chips and Swamp Dip (spicy corn chips and guacamole), Kentucky Saurus (thanks to the Colonel), Ceratops Garden (green salad), Dinosaur Eggs (boiled eggs gently cracked and soaked in beet juice, which when peeled are weird but beautiful), Prehistoric Mosquito Larvae in Amber (chewy snake or worm candy set in lemon gelatin); Misty, Marshy, Murky Abode of Cherriasaurus (creamy cherry dessert), Jurassic Gelatin (use the blue one); Dino Pops (anything frozen on a stick), Prehistoric Pie (any kind of pie), Triceratops Trifle (what else?), Strawberry Strata (any strawberry dessert), Elasmosaurus Pool (chocolate pudding).

HIPPOPOSTEROUS CHRISTMAS

It's preposterous to even think of celebrating
Christmas without honoring Christ

OPTIONS

Ladies' Evening
Family Fun Night
Kids' Christmas Party
Teens' Christmas Party
Couples' Party

DECORATIONS

Tables

Use rainbow colors for table coverings.

Centerpieces

Hippos and palm trees (decorate with tiny Christmas ornaments), surrounded by mounds of shredded ribbon in rainbow colors (See Resources.)

Room Decorations

Decorate walls with hippos in rainbow colors by enlarging pattern. (See Appendix, Items 4-A—4-E.)

Name Tags

Little rainbow-colored hippos. (See Appendix, Item 4-F.) Attach a colored paper clip to each one to be used in playing the game Watch What You Say.

Program Cover

(See Appendix, Item 4-G.)

Take-Home Favor

Hippo Christmas Tree Ornament (See Resources.)

SPECIAL FEATURES

Songs

"Take Me Out to the Ball Game" (See Resources.)
"The Old Gray Hair" (See Resources.)
"Oh, the Marlin; Oh, the Marlin" (See Resources.)

Demonstration

Festive jewelry made out of candy

Games

Watch What You Say (See Resources.)
Make a Word (See Resources.)
White "Hippo" Sale (instead of White Elephant) (See Resources.)

Gift

Hippo-Dippo (See Resources.)

DEVOTION

(See Resources.)

FOOD

Barbecued Hippo-Size Meatballs
Nutty Mushroom Rice
Roly-Poly Hippo-pie-tamus

RESOURCES

Centerpiece

Copy centerpiece pattern (see Appendix, Items 4-H, 4-I) onto multi-colored, marbled construction paper and cut out. Embellish all sides of palm branches with green glitter. Connect the ends so the hippos form a circle. Cut slits as indicated in palm branches, then attach the palm branches by slipping into slits on top of tree. Add round stickers or tiny ornaments to ends of palm branches for decoration.

Take-Home Favor

Hippo Christmas Tree Ornament

Copy onto multicolored, marbled construction paper. (See Appendix, Item 4-J.) Cut out circles and glue the backs of two together, placing a fine cord loop between the layers for a hanger. Using ¼" or ½" red satin ribbon, make small bows and glue to neck of hippos. Apply iridescent glitter paint to hippos for accent.

Songs

These three totally silly, off-the-wall songs are to be sung by the Happy Hippettes. Three people dressed in the style of your choice, but with very big, padded hips. For the first song they would also wear baseball hats and T-shirts with any number on the back in big figures. For the second song people with gray hair would make the song really special, and on the last line they will put on one of those brightly colored clown wigs from the toy store and then sing the song again. For the third song, the Hippettes should come out dressed in their favorite fishing gear.

Take Me Out to the Ball Game

(to the tune of the song with the same title)

by Nora Burdett and Karen Keller

Take me out to the ball game;
  Buy me a hot dog with kraut.
I'll have some popcorn and candy bars too;
  Please buy me plenty so I'll not run out.

Well, it's root, root, root beer and cola,
  Ice cream sundaes, oh shame.
Oh it's one, two, three, I got fat
  At the old ball game.

The Old Gray Hair
(to the tune of "The Old Gray Mare")
by Nora Burdett and Karen Keller

Oh, my old gray hair just ain't what it used to be,
Now I just don't look like me,
Feel like I have been set free.
My old gray hair just ain't what it used to be,
Someone did a job on me.

Oh, the Marlin; Oh, the Marlin
(to the tune of "O My Darlin' Clementine")
by Nora Burdett and Karen Keller

Oh, the marlin; oh, the marlin
That I caught out in the sea;
Oh he looked just like my darlin'
Who was lost down in Fiji.

Oh, the marlin; oh, the marlin;
Well I took him home with me.
Then I cooked him for my dinner,
But I got heartburn, you see!

Oh, the moral of this story,
Is that there will always be
A lot more darlin' marlins
Out there in the deep blue sea.

Demonstration

The Hippoposterous Festive Necklace

The demonstrator should be wearing one of the necklaces and chewing gumdrops as she talks and shows how they're made. She could even throw a piece of candy to the audience every so often. She should be dressed very festively, perhaps with a "wrapped candy decoration" in her hair as well. Have several necklaces already made up. Demonstrator should give directions with great enthusiasm, talking about the importance of color, length, type of candy, and the look you want. For example, "This will be the perfect gift to give this season . . . You can wear it and later eat it, then use what it is strung with to floss your teeth . . . It is a gift that just keeps on giving."

I. Supplies Needed

A. Dental floss for stringing necklace; bright cord or ribbon for necklace you tie candy onto.

B. Strong, medium to long, tapestry needle.

C. Candy (Candy must be soft enough to push a needle through or wrapped with a twist on each end so it can be securely tied.)

1. Gumdrops in bright colors, orange slices, and marshmallow bananas

2. Bite-sized, individually wrapped candy bars (for the chunky necklace)

3. Bubble gum

4. Sticks of gum wrapped in silver paper

5. Small candy canes

6. Any type of candy with a hole in the middle

II. Types of Necklaces to Talk About or Show

A. Chunky—using little candy bars

B. Jewel—using gumdrops

C. Chewy—using a stick of gum strung through one end interspersed with a small round candy

D. Candy cane

E. The chocolate lover's necklace—for that "melt on your dress, not in your hand" look

F. Wrapped candy necklace for those who like to be "heard," unwrapped for those who desire to nibble without disturbing those around them

(You are really only limited by your imagination.)

III. Directions

A. Measure dental floss string for necklace long enough to slip easily over the head.

B. Decide on which colors and types of candy to mix to give an appealing effect.

C. If you choose candies wrapped with twist on each end, tie candies onto a bright cord or ribbon.

It's so easy it's preposterous as well as being Hippoposterously wonderful.

Games

Watch What You Say

Choose a word that people won't be allowed to say for the evening, perhaps a slang word from your area that people tend to use too much. Some examples: yeah, na, nope, yep, huh?, um, uh-huh. Everyone should have a colored paper clip on her name tag. If you catch someone saying the forbidden word, you may take that person's paper clip and attach it to your name tag. If someone catches you saying the word, that person may take one of your clips. At the end of the night the person with the most paper clips wins. Now, watch what you say!

Make a Word

Pass out to everyone sheets of paper that you have copied or printed ahead of time with "HIPPOPOSTEROUS" written across the top. Have guests make as many words from it as they can in seven minutes.

White "Hippo" Sale

Like the old white elephant sale, have guests bring something from home that is still good but useless to them. You could auction them off among the guests and then use the money to help out a needy family for Christmas.

Gift

Hippo-Dippo

Have everyone bring the most preposterous gift they can find within a price range specified by you. It should be suitable for any age or sex. It must be wrapped in anything except traditional Christmas paper. Put all gifts in a large box and let each person draw from the gift box during the evening.

Devotion

What in the world do hippos, palm trees, baseball, and marlins have in common? Just about as much as some of the other things we find around at Christmas—absolutely nothing! They are totally unrelated.

Many things we do at Christmas sidetrack us from the real meaning of the events that make the season special.

1. The birth of the Savior has made a way for the entire world to be redeemed. Now that's worth celebrating! We may try to do something about our sinful condition by good works, religion, or philosophy. But that's preposterous! (Use the following Scripture references: Prov. 14:12; John 3:16; Rom. 5:8.)

2. Focus on what Christ has done for us. Then praise Him and share the good news with others. (Use the following Scripture references: Ps. 51:15; Luke 2:14; Ps. 9:11; Prov. 11:30; Dan. 12:3.)

3. Finish the program with the Christmas story and traditional Christmas carols.

Remember: It's Hippoposterous to Leave Christ Out of Christmas.

Food

Barbecued Hippo-Size Meatballs

Meatballs:

3 lbs. extra lean ground beef	1 can light evaporated milk
2 c. quick oats	2 eggs
1 chopped onion	½ tsp. garlic
2 tsp. salt	½ tsp. pepper
2 tbsp. chili powder	

Mix all ingredients together well. Shape into small baseball-size meatballs. Place in a large baking dish.

Sauce:

2 c. catsup	½ tsp. garlic powder
2 c. brown sugar	½ c. chopped onion
1 tbsp. liquid smoke	

Mix and bring to a boil. Pour over meatballs. Bake one hour at 350 degrees. Delicious. Quantity would serve about 8 men or 12 ladies.

Nutty Mushroom Rice

8 c. cooked brown rice
2 c. chicken or vegetable stock
24 mushrooms, sliced
4 spring onions, cut into ½" lengths
1 c. chopped pecan nuts (or walnuts, pine nuts, or a mixture)

Heat chicken or vegetable stock in large pan or wok. Cook mushrooms and onions in stock for 3 to 4 minutes. Add nuts and rice and toss while heating through. Serve hot or cold. Serves 16.

Roly-Poly Hippo-pie-tamus
(fat-free)

¾ c. sugar

1 c. water

2½ tsp. cinnamon

nonstick cooking spray

8 c. sliced, canned apples

20 6" flour tortillas

Preheat oven to 350 degrees and spray baking dish with fat-free cooking spray. Combine sugar and water in saucepan over medium heat, and stir until sugar is dissolved. Combine apples and cinnamon, mix well. Place ½ cup apple mixture down the center of each tortilla. Roll up each tortilla and place seam-side down in the baking dish. Pour sugar sauce over tortillas. Cover with foil and bake in preheated oven for 30 minutes. Remove foil and continue baking an additional 25 to 30 minutes. Delicious served with low-fat whipped topping or ice cream.

CIRCLES

Is your life like a vicious circle,
or do you have your priorities in order?

OPTIONS

Ladies' Evening or Day Seminar

Christian Workers' Evening or Day Seminar

Professionals' Party

Teen Night

DECORATIONS

Tables

Cover with brightly colored cloths. Place large sheet of white paper (2' x 3') in center of each table.

Centerpieces

Cut circles in various sizes and colors and lay on the white sheet of paper in center of each table. Using a hole punch, make lots of little circles out of the scraps and scatter these like confetti around the larger circles. These will all be used later in Game 4.

Program Cover

(See Appendix, Item 5-A.)

Name Tags

Cut brightly colored circles and write on names.

Room Decorations

Round balloons in bright colors on sticks or filled with helium. Also cut many sizes of circles in many bright colors (lightweight paper will do). Scatter lots of circles all over the floor of the meeting room. Don't worry about people stepping on them. They will be used later. Using large circles (about 12" diameter), cut out the letters to form the word "C—I—R—C—L—E—S" and decorate walls. (See Appendix, Item 5-B.)

SPECIAL FEATURES

Songs

"Let the Circle Be Broken" (See Resources.)

"God's Love Is like a Circle" (published by Child Evangelism Fellowship and available in Christian bookstores)

Poems

"Going in Circles"

Games

Circles in Your Possession (See Resources.)

How Many Circles Can You Think Of? (See Resources.)

Pick-up Circles (See Resources.)

Cut-ups (See Resources.)

Demonstration

Cut-up Cake (See Resources.)

Take-Home Favors

Circle Flower Bookmarks (See Resources.)

DEVOTION

Help! I'm Going in Circles (See Resources.)

FOOD

Light-as-a-Feather Cheese Ball (See Resources.)
Pecan Rounds (See Resources.)
Frozen Fruit Salad Ring (See Resources.)
Anything round: crackers, cheese balls, round sandwiches, cakes, cookies, and so forth

RESOURCES

Song

Let the Circle Be Broken
(to the tune of "Will the Circle Be Unbroken?")
by Nora Burdett and Karen Keller

Lord, today I feel more pressure,
And it comes from all around.
My duties pull me
This and that way,
So no balance I have found.

Oh, some circles should be broken;
Those that bind are not helpful.
Help me to focus
On what's important
And to grow in You and Your love.

Poem

Going in Circles
by Nora Burdett and Karen Keller

A circle is a thankless thing,
It has no beginning, nor end.
How did I get on?
Where do I get off?
When will this nightmare end?

My days are often like circles.
I seem to get so little done.
I rush around here,
And run around there,
Then find I haven't even begun.

Before I finish the ironing
I've started a dozen more tasks.
I've cleaned half the house,
I've started the wash.
Some order is all that I ask.

Soon I will pick up the children.
Their circles engulf me once more,
With music lessons and team sports,
Their youth group,
And oh, so much more.

I wonder if I should be working,
Or be involved in my community.
Then there's church—
with its vision and fervor.
I serve there with sincerity.

At the end of the day I'm exhausted.
No wonder love's flame has gone dim.
My husband and I
have grown strangers.
I do want to be there for him.

Teach me to listen to You, Lord,
Instead of running ahead.
Establish my ways,
Quiet my heart.
So the rest of my days I'll not dread.

Your love is just like a circle.
It goes on forevermore,
I will sing Your praise
Through all of my days,
And through eternity on heaven's shore.

Games

Circles in Your Possession

Award a prize to the guest with the most circles in his or her possession—for example, on clothes, in purse or wallet, in the form of jewelry, and so forth.

How Many Circles Can You Think Of?

Break into small groups and within a two-minute time limit have each group write down as many different things that are circles as they can think of. Compare answers of all groups and discard similar ones. The group with the most remaining original answers wins. (The prize should be something round, of course!)

Pick-up Circles

Have the guests race to see who can pick up the most circles on the floor. Voilá! You have a clean floor, and enough circles to use in the "cut-ups" game next. Give a prize for the person who picks up the most circles.

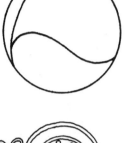

Cut-ups

Using the various circles on the white paper centerpieces, as well as the circles that have just been gathered off the floor, have each table of guests make a unique picture design out of nothing but the circles. They may be whole, cut, or folded and then glued to the white paper. Use as many of the circles as possible, either whole or cut up. You will need to supply scissors and glue or glue sticks for each group. (Some popular designs are: garden flowers, underwater scene, circus.) 15- to 20-minute limit.

Demonstration

Cut-up Cakes

Using one round, 8" or 9" cake layer you can make a wide variety of novelty cakes. Demonstrate the butterfly below. Helpful hint: If you freeze the cake before cutting and decorating, you will get neater cuts and less crumbs, and it will ice easier. Have fun. Decorate with jelly beans, coated chocolate candies, chocolate chips, licorice, nuts, and so forth.

Take-Home Favors

Circle Flower Bookmarks

Each favor requires 2 circles. Cut 2" circles from heavy construction paper, half of them from green and the other half from blue, pink, or yellow. On the latter colors print the verse "Matthew 22:37." Using a hole punch, make tiny circles from red construction paper. Use a fine black marker to make it look like a ladybug. Cut each green circle nearly in half and spread apart. Glue the verse circle on top of the green circle. The green circle becomes the leaves of the flower. On the back, near the bottom, glue a 10" piece of ½" green ribbon. Hide the glued end with a circle sticker. Glue ladybug to leaf on one side. Finish flower by painting on a transparent glitter paint.

Devotion

Help, I'm Going in Circles!

I. Women today seem to have more expected of them—they feel more pressure; more things are available to them; they are doing more in the Lord's work than ever before.

II. Bringing symmetry to the many circles of our lives would give us balance and order. The difficulty is fitting all the circles that demand so much into the time we have. It seems there are not enough hours in the day. Read 1 Chron. 29:15; Job 7:6; 9:25.

   A. We have many different circles—circles of family, husbands, children, home, church, needs of self, civic duties, work. (Illustrate with circles used on program cover. See Appendix, Item 5-A.)

   B. We need symmetry. Read Ps. 39:5; James 4:14. (See Appendix, Item 5-C.)

   C. We must redeem the time. Read Eph. 5:16; Col. 4:5; Ps. 90:12.

   D. Do we let the urgent come before the important? 1 Cor. 14:33.

44

III. Let's organize all our circles by prioritizing, using discipline, and making God the center. A love relationship with Him our first priority. Read Matt. 22:37. He and His Word will prioritize our world.

IV. How our circles of need, influence, and concern affect our priorities.

   A. Circle of need: this area must be met first. Each priority has special needs only you can fulfill. We have God's help in this awesome undertaking. Read Phil. 4:19.

   B. Circle of influence: this involves our attitude and example. Are you an encourager? A positive, joyful person? Read 2 Thess. 3:9; Titus 2:7; Heb. 11:4; James 5:10.

   C. Circle of concern: this involves the situations that weigh heavy on our hearts (i.e., the future, troubling circumstances, unfairness and heartache around us). Read 1 Pet. 5:7.

V. You must decide if you are going to take control of your life and time and give symmetry to your many circles. Read Matt. 6:24. We're either spiraling closer to the Lord and His plan for us or we're spiraling away and getting farther from His hand. Where are you?

To illustrate spirals, draw a circle about the size of a dinner plate. Make a cut around the edge of the circle, gradually spiraling into the center of the circle as the diagram shows. Hold from center of circle to represent spiraling upward to God. Hold outer edge of circle and let the spiral fall down to represent spiraling away from Him.

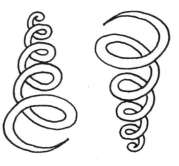

When scheduling a seminar, choose topics from these lists depending upon the group. Different speakers could offer sessions through the day and give the guests a choice of which to attend.

Ladies	*Teens*	*Professionals*
God	God	God
Husbands	Parents	Mate
Children	Friends	Family
Home	Home	Home
Church	Church	Church
Self	School	Self
Career	Work	Career
Activities Outside Home	Self	Social Life

Food

Light-as-a-Feather Cheese Ball

2 8-oz. pkgs. low-fat cream cheese or Neufchatel cheese
4-oz. jar pimento cheese spread
8 oz. low-fat sharp cheddar cheese
4 oz. blue cheese
4 oz. mozzarella cheese
2 tsp. Worcestershire sauce
2 tbsp. dried onion flakes
Coating choices: ½ c. chopped pecans; curry powder; paprika; chopped parsley; cracked pepper
   Combine room-temperature cheeses until well mixed, then form into 3 large balls. Roll each ball in your choice of the coatings above. Serve with crackers. Serves lots.

Pecan Rounds

1 c. butter or margarine
⅓ c. sugar
2 tsp. water
2 tsp. vanilla
2 c. flour
1 c. chopped pecans

Cream butter and sugar. Add 2 teaspoons water and vanilla; mix well. Blend in flour and chopped nuts. Chill 4 hours. Shape into balls. Bake on ungreased cookie sheet at 325 degrees for 20 minutes. Cool slightly and roll in confectioner's sugar. Makes about 3 dozen cookies.

Frozen Fruit Salad Ring

2 c. crushed pineapple (in juice, not syrup; save juice)
1 c. liquid (reserved juice plus water)
⅓ c. sugar
1 tbsp. flour
1 egg
8-oz package light cream cheese, softened
2 ½ c. miniature marshmallows
½ c. chopped red maraschino cherries, drained
1 can white seedless grapes, drained
3 ½ c. fruit cocktail, drained
½ c. pecans, finely chopped (optional)
1 c. whipped topping

Heat liquid to boiling. Combine sugar and flour; stir into egg. Remove liquid from heat. Add sugar mixture to hot liquid, stirring constantly. Boil 1 minute until thickened. Cool. In large bowl, blend cooled egg mixture and cream cheese. Stir in marshmallows, cherries, grapes, pineapple, and fruit cocktail. Fold in whipped cream. Divide mixture between two angel food cake pans or two gelatin ring molds or 24 muffin cups lined with paper baking cups. If desired, garnish with cherry halves. Freeze until firm, about 2 hours. Slice ½" to 1" thick (if cake pans or gelatin molds were used). Makes 18 to 24 servings.

TREASURES OF THE SEA

Seeing God's greatness in the treasures of the sea

OPTIONS

Family Fun Night
Ladies' Evening
Teens' Party
Kids' Party

DECORATIONS

Tables

Aqua tablecloths with peach accents. Use a rubber stamp with a shell motif to decorate napkins, cups, and so forth.

Centerpieces

Make a 4" to 6" wide wavy runner from butcher paper. Give the runner a sandy finish by either using a can of spray paint that gives the rough sandy texture, or by using a glue stick and running it randomly over the edges of the paper, then pour on fine sand and let dry. Place the runner down the center of the table. Scatter various shells and candles (freestanding or floating) along the runner.

Program Cover

Rubber stamp shells on aqua and peach paper to make covers

Name Tags

Rubber stamp shells on aqua and peach tags

Room Decorations

Jellyfish (See Resources.)
Walls could be decorated with nets, shells, and plastic or blow-up fish available at most craft and party stores

SPECIAL FEATURES

Songs

"Ship Ahoy"; "Throw Out the Lifeline"; "Rescue the Perishing"; "The Lighthouse"; "Peter, James and John Went Sailing in a Sailboat"; "Jonah, Jonah"; "I Will Make You Fishers of Men"; "Peace Be Still"; "Haven of Rest"; "God's Ocean of Love"

Games

Guess the Number of Shells (See Resources.)
Swimsuit Competition (See Resources.)
Sand Castles (See Resources.)
A Word with the Shells (See Resources.)
Seaside Tongue Twisters (See Resources.)

Skit

Pearl Perspective (See Resources.)

Demonstrations

Shell Angel Ornament (See Resources.)
Shell Pincushion (See Resources.)

Take-Home Favor Ideas

(See Resources.)

DEVOTION

God's Power over the Waves (See Resources.)

FOOD

Platter of various seafood nibbles
Seafood cocktails
Seafood and shell pasta casserole (See Resources.)
Curried shell pasta and seafood salad (See Resources.)

RESOURCES

Jellyfish Room Decorations

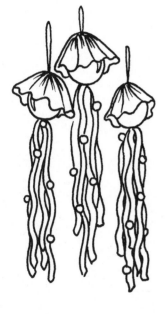

This beautiful jellyfish will be about 3 to 4 feet in length when finished.

Start with a clear balloon blown up nice and big. Attach clear fishing line to the tied opening of the balloon as a means of hanging the finished jellyfish. Cut a rounded, unevenly scalloped piece of very sheer, pale aqua, blue, or green chiffon big enough to cover two-thirds of the balloon. Attach to balloon by threading the fishing line through the chiffon to hold it in place so it can drape softly over the balloon. Cut eight ribbon or chiffon streamers in varying lengths and different shades of the aqua, blue, and green. Use a low-temp glue gun to attach the ribbons to the bottom of the balloon (jellyfish body.) Tie or hot glue at least five 2" plastic or glass balls randomly to the streamers (using only one ball on a streamer). Make at least three jellyfish and hang from the ceiling.

Games

Guess the Number of Shells

Fill a very large jar or glass container with as many shells as you can find (counting as you go), and set the container by the door. Upon entering, each person should guess how many shells it contains and write it on a piece of paper with his or her name. At the end of the program, announce the winner and award a prize.

Swimsuit Competition

Materials needed: bright tissue paper, scotch tape. Choose several teams to make old-fashioned swimsuits out of bright-colored tissue paper. Each swimsuit should be fashioned onto a member of each team.

Sand Castles

If you have access to sand, have several teams see who can make the best sand castle in the allotted time.

A Word with the Shells

Ten people should be chosen to carry pictures, which have been enlarged (see Appendix, Items 6-A—6-J) of different shells. On the back of the enlarged pictures, tape or glue a photocopy of the written segment about that particular shell. Each person will read the selection about that shell. Another person should be designated as the Seashell Seller, who will introduce each seashell. She should wear a large straw hat and carry a basket.

After the presentation, give guests a paper with the names of the shells and a brief description of each, mixed up, of course. Give them two minutes to match the shell and description. Provide a shell gift for the winner.

SEASHELL SELLER: Hello, I'm the Seashell Seller who sells seashells down by the seashore. Shells are actually the skeletons or houses of sea creatures called mollusks. If you have walked on a beach, you know that there are many kinds and shapes. Each shell is unique, with delicate patterns etched in soft colors on many different types and shapes. Each is important in God's plan. Let's meet a few of the shells now.

   One of the shells I sell is the cone shell.

1. Hello, I am a **cone shell,** and I can be very beautiful . . . but I am unique in that I am capable of killing my prey by injecting a poison through the tiny teeth on the end of my tongue. Watch out for me. If you touch me, you may be sorry. (Yellow, brown, salmon, or brown speckled.)

SEASHELL SELLER: I also sell scallop shells down by the sea.

2. I am a **scallop,** and I am pleased to say one of the jet set of the sea. I have 30 or more eyes to see where I am going, and I can travel where I please very quickly, until someone catches me and puts me on the dinner table. (White, brown, gray, or yellow.)

SEASHELL SELLER: If you were a butterfly, I would sell you, too, you see.

3. I am the beautiful **butterfly shell.** Though I can't fly, I am colored like the wings of a fragile butterfly. I stay hinged and spread my wings open only in death. Then I look like a fallen butterfly lying on the beach. (Delicate rainbow hues.)

SEASHELL SELLER: At the seashore my pen shells sell really well.

4. I am called a **pen shell** or **sea pen** because I look much like an old-fashioned quill pen people used to write with. I really can't write, but I am really good to eat. (Olive brown.)

SEASHELL SELLER: You'll find that I also sell cockleshells, that's for sure.

5. I am a **cockleshell** or heart shell as I am often called. "Mary, Mary, quite contrary" is said to have grown me in her garden. Isn't that a laugh! We all know I live in the sea. Molly Malone of Dublin sold me for food because I am a real tasty treat. (Red, orange, purple, or yellow.)

SEASHELL SELLER: Angel wings are seashells I sell on the shore.

6. I am known as the **angel wing** because of my shape. Even though I am fragile, I can use my rough edge to twist and turn and bore a hole in a solid rock big enough to hold myself. On the beach you will usually find only one side of me. (White.)

SEASHELL SELLER: I might have sold you a cuttlefish at my seashell shop.

7. I am a **cuttlefish,** and I am another of the jet set shell creatures of the same family as the octopus and squid. I can go backward and forward by drawing and squeezing water through my siphon.

My shell is used all over the world for a nutritional supplement for caged birds. (White.)

SEASHELL SELLER: One of the shells sold at my store on the shore is the ribbed triton.

8. I am a **ribbed triton** known as the musical instrument of the sea. I can be used as a trumpet and make a deep tone that can be heard for a long distance. (Brown.)

SEASHELL SELLER: If you want a conch shell, see me at the seashell shop.

9. I am the sought after **conch shell**. Even though I am a big, thick, heavy shell, I have a unique way of moving from one place to another. I raise myself up high and topple over again and again. (Pink.)

SEASHELL SELLER: The wentletrap is the last of the shells from my seashell shop.

10. I am a **wentletrap shell**, a Dutch name for the staircase I resemble. I come in many sizes and colors. (Salmon.)

ALL THE SHELLS: We are all unique and very special, and you are too. God made you special and has a plan for each of you.

Seaside Tongue Twisters

She sells seashells on the seashore.
The shells she sells are seashells, I'm sure.
So if she sells seashells on the seashore,
I'm sure she sells seashore shells.

Shellfish are sometimes smelt.
Smelt are surely not shellfish.
How selfish of a shellfish to think it is smelt.

Silly Sam should've swam,
Swiftly seeking shelter
From sleek sharks and slimy squid.
Sam should have surely shuddered.

If seashells are to sell,
Shall seashell sellers sell them?
Surely seashells should stay on the seashore.

Skit

Pearl Perspective
by Nora Burdett and Karen Keller

Cast: GRACE
SALLY
JENNA

Setting: Three friends are out for lunch in a café. Grace has just returned from a vacation in Hawaii, eager to share with her friends what she learned on her trip.

Props: Table, 3 chairs, 3 glasses of water, 2 small gift boxes with a "pearl" inside each (one from an inexpensive broken necklace will work fine), and a pearl ring on GRACE's hand.

(Two friends are seated at a table, and the vacationer walks in. She is greeted wildly by her two friends and sits down between them. She places her right hand into the middle of the table to show off a new pearl ring she is sporting.)

SALLY: Oh, my goodness. Look at that ring.

JENNA: Grace, what in the world? Couldn't you have found a bigger pearl?

GRACE: Isn't it just the most beautiful thing you've ever seen? I just knew you guys would love it.

SALLY: The only thing more beautiful than that would be the bucks it took to buy it.

GRACE: Oh, it wasn't that bad! Let me tell you about it.

JENNA: Oh boy, do we get to see the vacation video too?

GRACE: You might have to wait to see the video, but I can tell you some interesting things about pearls. For instance, do you know that pearls actually come from living organisms?

SALLY: Yeah? We have lots of things at my house that come from living organisms: colds, flu . . .

JENNA: . . . athlete's foot! *(Both ladies giggle and then quiet down as GRACE glances impatiently at each one.)*

GRACE: You see, there was this tall, handsome Polynesian diver *(both ladies lean forward to show increased interest now)*, and he was selling oysters from this big container. "Pick an oyster, you're guaranteed to find a pearl," the ad said. Well, this was our second honeymoon . . .

SALLY: You mean your fourth or fifth *(gives a little laugh)*.

GRACE: I think I got the biggest pearl of the day because even the diver looked shocked when he opened the oyster. Jim took it and had it set for me for our anniversary.

SALLY and JENNA: Ooo, now that's really romantic.

GRACE: Now, let me finish telling you what I learned about pearls. They are formed when a foreign object, like a grain of sand, gets into the oyster and causes an irritation.

SALLY: Oh yeah, Sammy had one of those in his ear the other day.

JENNA: What, a grain of sand or a pearl?

SALLY: No, silly. A foreign object!

GRACE *(sighs):* Now, once the grain of sand is in the oyster, it secretes layer after layer of mother-of-pearl, which envelops the irritation and makes it more bearable for the oyster. This process usually takes about four years before the precious pearl is at the right size to be harvested.

SALLY: Well, that must be what makes Sammy so precious. It has taken nearly four years to potty train that kid. *(Both ladies laugh again.)*

GRACE: Get serious, now, I'm trying to increase your not-so-vast storehouse of knowledge.

JENNA: That makes . . . (GRACE *looks at her over the top of her glasses, and she decides to be quiet.)*

GRACE: The last little tidbit I have about pearls is that they are the only gem that is of no value when broken.

SALLY: Well, if that were so at my house, nothing would have any value because just about everything I have is either chipped or broken. *(Shrugs her shoulders slightly)*

GRACE *(annoyed)*: Oh, you two are impossible! I have a good mind not to give either of you the present I brought you. *(Looks resolutely ahead while the two friends begin to beg and plead)*

SALLY and JENNA *(talking all over each other)*: Oh, please, please. We'll be good. We'll listen. We won't even try to be funny. We're sorry. Please forgive us. Did you really bring us a present, huh, huh?

GRACE: Yes, I did, but you two won't appreciate the gifts I brought you, because you haven't heard a word I've said.

SALLY and JENNA *(more pleading; talking over each other)*: Yes, we will. And we did listen. There was something about foreign objects and irritations and tall, handsome Polynesian divers. Yes, we got that part. Come on, Grace, what did you bring us?

GRACE: Well, not that you deserve them, but here. *(Gives them each a small box)*

SALLY: Oh, my goodness. It's a pearl.

JENNA: You got us a pearl. Oh, Grace, thank you, thank you.

GRACE: Well, they aren't as big as this one, and they will have to be set, but I thought they would be something special for each of you. Jenna, I think of all the difficult times you have had with your boss. I have seen you nearly at your wits' end many times. I know he is a real irritation to you, just like that little grain of sand in the oyster. And, Sally, I know that dealing with doctors and trying to find help for Sammy's disabilities has many times given you untold irritations. But, girls, what I want you to remember is that God has given you these little seeds of irritation, and others, too, no doubt. You may not be able to do much about the problems you are facing, but the Lord has allowed you to have them for a purpose, and He will make them tolerable. Just think of these irritations as pearls of patience in the making.

SALLY: I just wish the pearls of patience only took four years to form like the real ones. But I'm afraid we might both be working on our pearls for a long time.

GRACE: My dear friends, I think that most of the pearls God is making in our lives will take a lifetime.

Demonstrations

Shell Angel Ornaments

1. Obtain shells shaped so that they will serve as the dress of the angel.
2. Use a bead for the head. Make sure the head is in proper proportion to the size of the shell. A general rule is that the bead diameter should be about ⅓ of the length of the shell.
3. Use clear, iridescent paper twist for wings. Cut with pinking shears. Cut in length about 1½ times the width of the shell.
4. Open ribbon and tie in the middle. Flatten and shape into wings.
5. Tie a 7", thin, gold cord over the previous tie, making sure that the ends are even and the tie is positioned where the wings flair out.

6. Thread both ends of the cord through the bead. These ends will become the hanger for the angel.

7. Flatten the wing as it lies on a table, and attach the shell to the wing with hot glue.

8. Position the bead head at the top of the shell dress and attach with hot glue. A bow can cover any excess glue holding the head on.

9. Add a gold chenille wire for a halo. Tie the ends of the gold cord for hanging.

10. Draw closed eyes and an oval or heart-shaped mouth, and your angel is finished.

Shell Pincushions

Materials needed:
Lovely shells with a reasonably deep cavity
Stuffing (polyester fiberfill will work)
Satin material in soft shell colors like aqua, peach, pink, beige

Instructions:

1. Choose the satin that accents your shell best.

2. On a piece of paper turn your shell over and draw around it. Add 1" to the circumference, making another line. Use this as your pattern to cut the satin.

3. Cut satin and hand gather all around the edge of the pattern, pulling the threads to form a place to fill with stuffing. Pack firmly.

4. Fit the satin cushion into the shell cavity to see if more stuffing is needed. The cushion should be fairly firm and curve above the height of the shell.

5. When the cushion is right for the shell, tie off your gathering thread.

6. Hot-glue the cushion into the shell, making sure the glue is distributed evenly around a short distance from the edge and sufficient glue is in the bottom.

7. Add a satin cord between the cushion and the shell to give it a finished look if necessary.

Take-Home Favor Ideas

One shell soap and two bath oil beads, OR three bath oil beads in a shell, OR three pieces of saltwater taffy. Wrap in peach and/or aqua tulle and tie with contrasting ribbon.

Devotion

God's Power over the Waves

Introduction: Our world seems without direction. Circumstances are beyond our control. Sometimes we forget that we have a great God who is all-powerful.

I. At the seashore we can see the truth of God's greatness.

   A. He created the great seas and set their limits (Job 26:10; Isa. 51:15; Jer. 5:22).

   B. The waves display the mighty power of God.

      1. The waves are so powerful. They pound constantly and relentlessly with authority at the shoreline, reshaping the coastlines of great continents.

2. Waves sculpt rocks and hurl great logs upon the beach as if they were toothpicks. Even the sand of the seashore has been created by the crushing blows and endless flow of the tides. When the sea is peaceful, lapping gently to the shore, we know it is power under control.

II. Our lives ebb and flow as an ocean. Our emotional ups and downs are like the tides of our being. Great storms often come into our lives in powerful waves.

A. Waves of tumult. These waves are stressful emotionally and mentally and make us feel agitated and disturbed. The noise of these waves is deafening and prevents us from making proper decisions and assessments.

B. Waves of trouble. These are unfortunate circumstances and misfortunes that come into our lives. They can be overwhelming, bringing great distress, pain, and worry. God can still these waves and bring peace (Ps. 107:25-29; John 16:33; Isa. 43:2).

C. Waves of anger. Anger many times rushes over us like a raging wave. It is devastating to others and us. God can still that wave (Ps. 89:9; 37:8; Prov. 14:17).

III. Do you have a personal relationship with the powerful God who created the seas and can control the waves? **Are you letting Him calm and control the waves in your life?**

Food

Seafood and Shell Pasta Casserole

10 oz. shell pasta, uncooked
2 tbsp. water
½ medium onion, chopped
1 clove garlic
1 c. skim milk
2 tsp. cornstarch
½ green pepper, chopped
¼ c. grated Parmesan cheese
1½ c. mixed cooked seafood, or crabmeat, chopped
1 tbsp. parsley, chopped
black pepper and salt to taste

Fill large saucepan two-thirds full with water, and bring to a boil. Add pasta and boil rapidly for 10 to 12 minutes until tender, but firm.

Prepare sauce: Boil two tablespoons water. Add onion and garlic and cook until tender. In a small bowl, blend 1 tablespoon milk with the cornstarch to make a smooth paste. Stir in the remainder of the milk. Add mixture to the onion and garlic, and stir constantly over medium heat until sauce thickens.

Over medium heat, add all the remaining ingredients, and stir to combine and heat through. Drain the pasta and add to the sauce. Toss gently to combine. Serve at once.

Curried Shell Pasta and Seafood Salad

1½ c. uncooked shell pasta
½ c. diced celery
4 green onions

2 tbsp. raisins
¼ c. green and red bell pepper, diced
2 tbsp. parsley, chopped
½ c. sweet corn kernels
¾ c. crab meat, chopped

In boiling water cook noodles for 10 to 12 minutes until tender but firm. Combine noodles with remaining ingredients. Toss in dressing and refrigerate one hour before serving.

Dressing:
½ c. low-fat natural yogurt
2 tsp. curry powder
2 tbsp. chopped parsley
1 clove garlic, minced

Mix all ingredients and season to taste. Chill. Best if used the same day.

Appendix

SCHEDULE FOR PLANNING A BANQUET OR PARTY

Three Months Before

1. Pray.
2. Choose theme and date.
3. Set budget
4. Choose speaker and issue invitation.
5. Choose and secure location.
6. Organize function committees and plan details.

   a. Decorations and colors

   b. Special features (skits, songs, readings, plays, poems, puppets, games, crafts, demonstrations)

   c. Food (If using caterers, see when they need the final number of guests. Set menu. Do they provide table coverings and setups? Will you have waiters and/or waitresses or serve buffet style?)

   d. Baby-sitters (You may need to be willing to pay for this service or exchange services with members of another local church.)

   e. Fees, gifts, acknowledgments (for speaker, soloists or other guest performers, committee chairmen, and so forth.)

   f. Publicity (posters, church buulletin, newspaper, local businesses, etc.)

   g. Sound (public address system, various microphones, and taping or videoing)

   h. Cleanup

One Month Before

1. Reconfirm location reservations.
2. Encourage and remind speaker. See if he or she has any special needs or requirements. Make arrangements for his or her transportations and/or accommodation.
3. Check on committee leaders.
4. Set date for ticket sales (approximately two weeks before event).
5. Don't forget to pray!

On the Day

1. Leaders and committee members arrive early.
2. Attend to last-minute decorations (set out flowers and so on.)
3. Check sound system and recording equipment.
4. Set out glass of water for speaker.
5. Be sure honorarium is prepared for speaker and is in proper hands.
6. Go over order of events to make sure everything runs smoothly.
7. Relax before arrival of guests.

SCHEDULE FOR PLANNING A RETREAT

Six Months Before

1. Pray.
2. Choose theme and date.
3. Set budget
4. Choose speaker and issue invitation.
5. Choose and secure location.
6. Plan details.
   a. Decorations and colors
   b. Special features
   c. Devotions
   d. Food
   e. Baby-sitters
   f. Fees

Two Months Before

1. Reconfirm location reservations.
2. Encourage and remind speaker.
3. Organize function committees (have a leader in each section).
   a. Decorations
   b. Special features
   c. Food
   d. Registration
   e. Cleanup
   f. Baby-sitters

One Month Before

1. Have prayer times.
2. Increase publicity, begin to sell tickets, and make reservations
3. Meet with committee leaders.

One Week Before

1. Check with each committee member.
2. Order flowers or fruit basket for speaker's room.
3. Finalize attendance numbers with caterers and retreat facility.

On the Day

1. Leaders and committee members arrive early.
2. Attend to last-minute decorations (set out flowers and so on.)
3. Check sound system and recording equipment.
4. Set out glass of water for speaker.
5. Be sure honorarium is prepared for speaker and is in proper hands.
6. Go over order of events to make sure everything runs smoothly.
7. Relax before arrival of guests.

fold

Item 1-B

Item 1-C

Item 1-D

FOR BERRIES (Complete at least four or five of these thoughts to be shared with your special Blossom.)

I AM . . .

I LIKE . . .

I THINK . . .

I COULD GIVE . . .

I UNDERSTAND . . .

I WILL . . .

I COULD SHARE . . .

I REMEMBER . . .

I WOULD LIKE CHRIST TO . . .

I WONDER . . .

Item 1-E

FOR BLOSSOMS (Complete at least four or five of these thoughts to be shared with your special Berry.)

I AM . . .

I LIKE . . .

I THINK . . .

I FEAR . . .

I FEEL . . .

I WISH . . .

I WOULD LIKE CHRIST TO . . .

I WOULD LIKE TO LEARN . . .

I DREAM . . .

I NEED . . .

Item 1-F

Berry Special Friends

Mentoring Ministry of _____ **(name of your church)** _____

Name _____

Address _____ City _____ Zip _____

Phone (Home) _____ (Work) _____

Work Schedule _____

Single _____ Married _____ Divorced _____ Widow _____

Number of Children _____ Ages and Sex of Children _____

_____

How long have you been a Christian? _____

Tell about how you were saved? _____

_____

_____

_____

_____

What do you like to do? _____

_____

What are your life goals at this time? _____

_____

Tell about any outstanding events in your life apart from your salvation. _____

_____

_____

_____

On a scale of 1 to 5 (1 being a quiet life, 5 being extremely busy) how would you rate your life right now? _____

What do you feel is the greatest need in your life now? _____

_____

_____

Item 2-A

Proverbs Quiz

METAPHOR

1. Honeycomb (16:24)

2. A word fitly spoken (25:11)

3. Cold snow in the time of harvest (25:13)

4. Clouds and wind without rain (25:14)

5. A broken tooth; a foot out of joint (25:19)

6. A city that is broken down, without walls (25:28)

7. A dog returns to its own vomit (26:11)

8. Take a dog by the ears (26:17)

9. A continual dropping on a rainy day (27:15)

10. A ruler who oppresses the poor (28:3)

MEANING

A. Meddling in business not belonging to you

B. Confidence in an unfaithful man

C. A man with no self control

D. A fool returns to his folly

E. A quarrelsome woman

F. A sweeping rain that leaves no food

G. Pleasant words

H. Precious gift of gold and silver

I. A faithful messenger

J. A person without the gift he or she claims to have

Item 2-C

I Wish

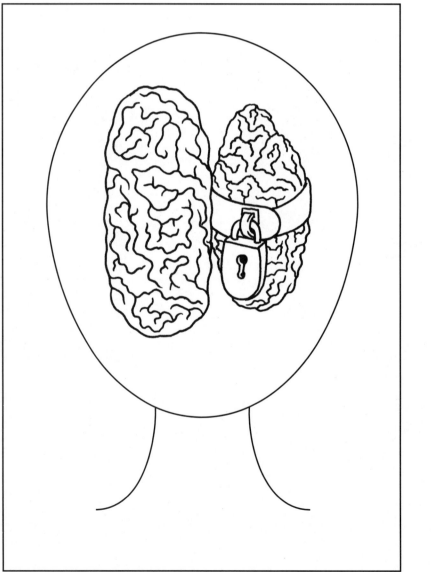

Time-Release
Creativity Boosters

Dino-mite
at _____

Item 4-A

Item 4-B

Item 4-C

Item 4-D

Item 4-E

Item 4-F

Hippoposterous Christmas

—the most preposterous Christmas party you've ever seen—

HELP! I AM RUNNING IN CIRCLES, CIRCLES, CIRCLES!

NEEDS

HUSBAND

GOD

DEVELOPING A LOVE RELATIONSHIP WITH HIM

ACTIVITIES OUTSIDE HOME

SELF

INFLUENCE

CONCERNS

CHURCH

CHILDREN

HOME

WORK

These represent 12" circles that will be cut out into the word.

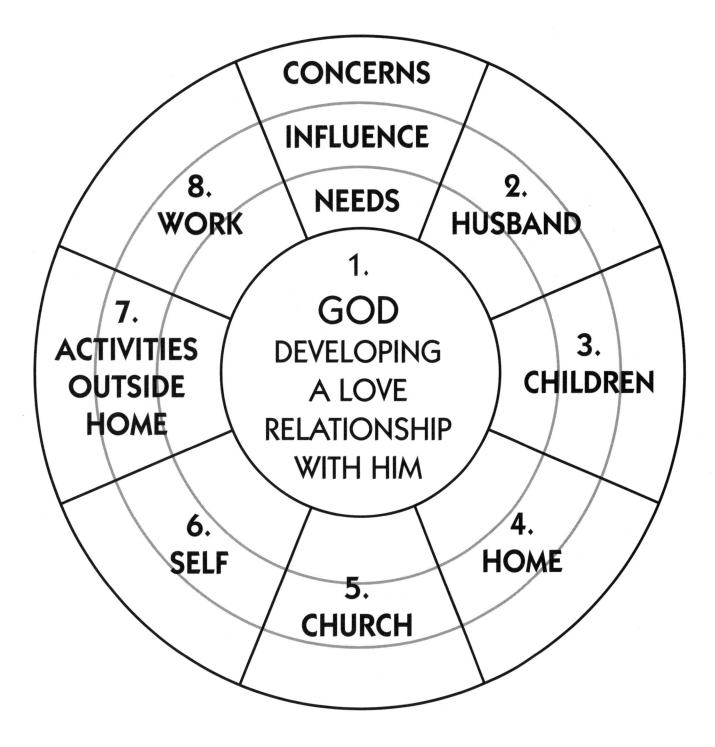

Item 6-A

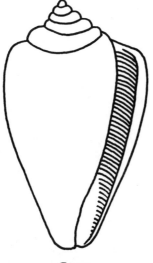

Cone

Item 6-B

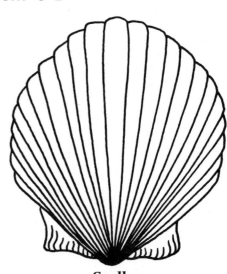

Scallop

Item 6-C

Butterfly

Item 6-D

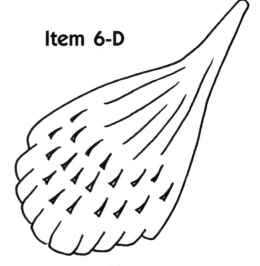

Pen Shell (or Sea Pen)

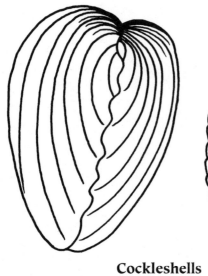

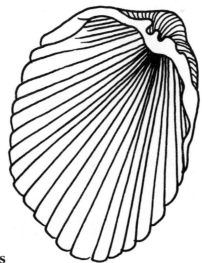

Cockleshells

Item 6-E

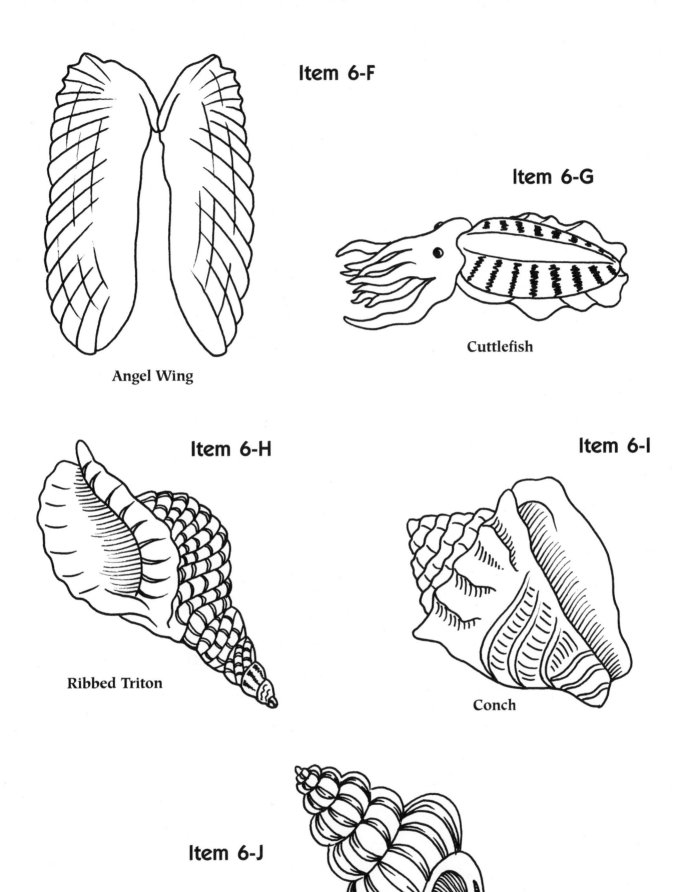

Item 6-F

Angel Wing

Item 6-G

Cuttlefish

Item 6-H

Ribbed Triton

Item 6-I

Conch

Item 6-J

Wentletrap (or Staircase)

Bibliography

Berry Special Friends

Brestin, Dee. *The Friendships of Women*. Colorado Springs: Chariot Victor Publication, 1997.

Kraft, Vicki. *Women Mentoring Women: Ways to Start, Maintain, and Expand a Biblical Women's Ministry*. Chicago: Moody Press, 1992.

Circles

Barnes, Emilie. *More Hours in My Day*. Eugene, Oreg.: Harvest House Publishers, 1994.

———. *Survival for Busy Women*. Eugene, Oreg.: Harvest House Publishers, 1994.

Creative Encounter

Hanks, Kurt and Jay Parry. *Wake Up Your Creative Genius*. Menlo Park, Calif.: Crisp Publications, Inc., 1991.

Von Oech, Roger. *A Whack on the Side of the Head: How You Can Be More Creative*. New York: Warner Brothers, Inc., 1990.

Treasures of the Sea

Withers, C., comp. *A Rocket in My Pocket: The Rhymes and Chants of Young Americans*. Holt, 1948.

Index